Shattered Dreams

A Girl Named Silas and Me

Susan Peterson Lane

abbott press®

A DIVISION OF WRITER'S DIGEST

Abbott Press books may be ordered through booksellers or by contacting:

Abbott Press
1663 Liberty Drive
Bloomington, IN 47403
www.abbottpress.com
Phone: 1-866-697-5310

ISBN: 978-1-4582-1332-7 (sc)
ISBN: 978-1-4582-1331-0 (e)

Library of Congress Control Number: 2013922697

Printed in the United States of America.

Abbott Press rev. date: 01/27/2014

Contents

Foreword

Little Girl Lost

Little Girl Lost.
Little Girl tossed in a world of despair.
Does anybody care about Little Girl Lost?

Little Girl Lost had bad mother, worse father, or the reverse
life perverse, utterly destroyed by 3.
Little eyes to see drugs/guns, often hungry and cold in much pain
with great shame.
Little Girl Lost.

Little Girl Lost raped and ruined by 7.
Hardened to Life's problems and rebellious by 11.
Little Girl Lost.

Little Girl Lost.
Doll less and Joyless. Living/Creating a Fantasy that will
never be.
Little Girl Lost.

Little Girl Lost.
Grows in time, wrong friends acquired, before she
understands what not to do.
Little Girl Lost.

Little Girl Lost, thought I know.
I'll have a child, who will love me, fulfill me and supply my needs.
Perhaps, even heal my pain. Wrong again, misconception, children
take not give what they need to live.
Little Girl Lost.

Little Girl Lost said I know a man. This will work.
Not Sam, maybe John, Jimmy or Kenny, Richard or Benny.
At such cost to self, stripped of her Dignity.
Little Girl Lost.

Little Girl Lost thought now this must work.
I've found a home, I've found the Church. Rev. Johnson, Sister
Harkins, or Elder Smiley will help you know.
Wrong again. Traps there in, new snares, yet another child, new
wounds, more pain, no gain.
Little Girl Lost.

Little Girls Lost.

Not all were born into affliction for some old wealth, not new stealth, hidden sins, no less grim.

Some public figures, groomed and pampered, indulged not hampered by physical lack.

Surely, money kept their lives in tack.

Yet we still see Little Girls Lost some far worse than you or me.

Little Girl Lost thinks. Yes, I've arrived.

Prominence is mine, I've escaped, respect I've gained.

I've a degree, nice home, well dressed is me. New car, I've traveled seen new places, been to an island or three.

Little Girl Lost can't be me.

Little Girl Lost.

Born of a dynasty, a political figure with power and acclaim or the movie star with money and fame says

Little Girl Lost is not my name.

Little Girl Lost.

Rich and Poor alike think I'm married all is ok even with adulterous mates and wayward children. The pain is still there yet to abate.

Little Girl Lost is still your fate.

Little Girl Lost.

Now 70 plus 7, little time left but to ponder.

Few days, old ways, past mistakes, rights done, wrongs won.

Little Girl Lost can that be thee?

Little Girl Lost.

The pills, the smack, the bottle, the crack won't make it right.

Won't cause the pain to flee.

Little Girl Lost is yet you ,yet me.

Little Girl Lost.

Black, Asian, Hispanic or White.

Where can you be happy?

Where can you be free?

The answer is not in a person, a place or a thing.

It is only at the foot of the Cross that

Little Girl Lost is Finally Found.

Amen.

Introduction

There is a triumph born of tragedy and trauma. There is a peace born of pain. And there is an upright walk born of diligence, perseverance amid failure and defeat. The whys, the wheres, the hows and whens are often dictated by the choices that we make in our lives. Challenges and Difficulty are a given. And as surely as we are born we will die but what we do in the in between times does matter. For we all have a legacy within us to leave. Our lives usually speak our choices and our words; speak our thoughts, desires and feelings at points in our time(s). Shattered Dreams speaks of my thoughts and feelings at a point in my life.

Dedication

Called from complacency

Compelled to change

Challenged to write

By Christ the Light

Dedicated to the Greater Glory of God

Catharsis

I awoke one morning much to my chagrin and I noticed
that I had survived and I asked myself why?
Disaster had struck, the storm had hit, the barriers
were crossed and yet I had survived.

Immediately, I told myself that this was a bad dream.
I will wake up soon and it will all be over.
This nightmare is not part of my life.
It is not welcomed.
I did not invite it in.
And after all, I did nothing to deserve this.
But as the days passed, I began to realize that I would
not die, I could not die (for I had responsibilities).
More importantly, I began to realize that I was not
alone and my acceptable lifestyle did not exempt
me from problems, pain, and suffering.
I came to know that I was part of the larger
we who had survived.

bad childhoods, broken relationships, misplaced loyalties,

survived

shattered dreams, damaged self-esteem, empty promises

survived

despair, discouragement and disappointments

survived

unexpected/unwanted pregnancies, wayward

children, unfaithful mates, broken marriages,

survived

cruel hoaxes, alcoholism, drug addiction, and immorality

survived

immaturity, irresponsibility, impulsiveness

survived

physical abuse, mental abuse, emotional abuse

survived

helplessness, hopelessness, hypocrisy, and hypertension

survived

mistake after mistake after mistake

survived

untold indignities, told indignities and other deficiencies

survived

embarrassment and sufferings that penetrated

to the core of our soul

marred our outlook and colored our attitudes and dispositions

to the point that we were almost but not quite unreachable,

unteachable and undeliverable but we survived

out of necessity to become

unshakable, immovable and indomitable

we survived

to hear that still small voice within

say arise pick up your cross and follow me daily

we survived

to the can'ts became cans, the don'ts became

do's and the won'ts became wills.

WE SURVIVED.

Chaos

Numerous Nights

Countless Hours

Spent alone teeming with tears,

Waiting, worrying (that you might be dead).

Listening for the familiar engine sound

Hour after hour waiting for the key to unlock the door.

Then finally a click in the quiet of the night,

Then instant relief (because you were well.)

Followed by my foolish desires to believe your explanation(s)

knowing full well that ne'er word uttered was true.

Yet numb I arise.

The lies are no longer acceptable.

The excuses will no longer due.

Your selfish quest for happiness woven in a tangled web of

deception and lies has proven too costly for all involved.

You've imbibed of your own desires far too long.

Your privileges are gone.

Now

You stand alone, exposed and naked yet still full of
the stench of the Pride that caused your fall.
Know that I am not your Accuser.
I speak only the truth from the issues of my heart.
And how do I stand against the pity party of despair
for anger, bitterness and pain abide within,
Discussion is ineffectual for you see only with
tunnel vision what was that no longer is.
Where do we go from here?
Or is it where do I go from here?
Is restoration possible?
Is it desirable?
And yet we know not the end.

You are not the Alpha.
Nor I the Omega.
TRUTH beckons us to stand still.
Wait and see if but for a moment in time.

5

Castaways

Homeless and Deprived, aborted and alive
Runaways hopping trains.
Do we dare ignore their pain?

Downtrodden in despair,
Broken beyond repair.
Dirty and neglected.
Can we see life from their perspective?

MOTHERLESS, FATHERLESS, and GODLESS indeed,
They suffer with constant and irrepressible needs.

Drug-addicted and alcohol-driven
Chasing ghosts that remain hidden to the naked eye.

But this is the 2000th year,
Can we leave our sisters in despair?

We are each of us called to care enough, to
bare and share in their repair.
The invitation remains open. Will they be made whole?

Condemned

STOP! DO NOT ENTER IN!
This dwelling is condemned.
The main frame is cracked, the steel beams are
bent, and the iron gates are rusted.
STOP! DO NOT ENTER IN!

DO NOT ENTER IN!
Too many promises were broken, too many lies spoken.
The symbol of love was stolen. You just can't come in.

What remains is hurt and pain,
emptiness, loneliness and often shame.
The dwelling is just not the same.
Try not to enter.
Condemnation lies within!

Consequences

(Incomplete and Uncut)

Who are you? Samson?

Where did you come from? Samson?

Where is the money? Panderer.

Know ye not the truth? Liar.

What do you want of me? Samson?

You've hurt me.

You've betrayed me.

And I deny you re-entry into my world.

Your tears no longer move me.

Your guilt no longer pleases me.

You have not even the presence of mind to say I'm sorry.

You claim to love me.

I do not want even to remember you.

I do not recognize you.

But wait, you do look vaguely familiar.

Oh yes, I did know you once but I've chosen to forget you.

I've grown comfortable without you.

A Do Not Disturb sign now guards my heart.

Since you went to the party and refused to come away.

Now you are infected, your mind is clouded.

And it's too late my faithless, faceless former friend.

Yet, despite where you've gone, and all you've done,

my hope is that the 3 R's of

rebirth, rejuvenation and restoration renew the man within you.

Climb Blind

I took a spill down an uphill walk.
How much would it take to get back up?
More than I had or knew I possessed.

I was bruised, scratched, chaffed, and dazed.
Part human, part crazed.

I felt much pain, some shame,
Too old to fall let alone
crawl along blind-sided
by the attractive rose bush
with thorns too prickly to touch.
But thought I, I must.

Wrong choice.

Damn hard ride.

I lay there awhile before I realized

I fell in a muddy pit.

Before long, I began to sink and stink.

My gut erupted,

My head pounded,

My bowels loosened,

And I could not see.

Then I heard two words

Climb Blind.

No money, no funds,

No friends, no job,

Bad man, no plan

Climb Blind.

No home, no phone,
Five kids, one room
Climb blind.

No food, years lost,
Can't walk, can't talk,
Too hard to think,
All wrong.

Climb Blind
To meet He who alone
Can resurrect you and me.

Eternity at a Glance

I've only a glimpse to share
Only a moment to spare
To relay the simple truth
I've not died, I'm alive,
Living just beyond your
Reach, on the other side.

Now I sit at the Master's feet
And rest. No more trials,
No more tests.

Permanent Peace is mine.
No more do I fear, I'm fine.
Just on the other side.

So I bid you not goodbye but hello,

Rejoice with me.

Finally, all else has passed.

At home at last.

As folk would say,

I'm here, I've arrived

On the other side to stay.

Mourn not my departure.

I'm not lost to you.

Just housed now on the other side of through.

P.S. I'll see you again.

The Broken Bike

When just a tike
You had a broken bike
Often too little coal
with old, little clothes.
Chicken pox, mumps, and hospital stays;
A favorite toy once taken away.

Labeled from birth a factory worker,
Commoner, no future but dirt.
But you defied the labels and the lies.

You moved forward.

Focused on change.

You tasted progress.

Ne'er to remain the same.

You do remember with some regrets

But it is not over, the end not yet.

2013 will usher you from the cycle of Hell.

The chains will loosen, the shackles fall off,

Just believe and receive

The better half of the new call.

Accept the invitation,

Embrace the change.

The choice, a simple YES

to a new and permanent way.

The Anatomy of a Prayer

Reel to Real

No practiced words

Just honesty, humility, and a sprinkling of zeal.

Sit, Stand, or Kneel.

It matters not the position of the flesh,

But the posture of the heart.

Compare your approach

Not to a another. It is

Not a competition, or art

But the conversation

We have the privilege to start apart

From the external.

Don't imitate duplicate
or steal. Only sincerity
and honesty will do.

Have a thought.
Take a Care.
How can you give less?

Reel to Real
Your prayer must be
where you are, not what
you think or how you feel.

The Plump She

The Plump She
A broken heart, a rusty key,
Is she you or is it me?

Or is it the third word? The thin her.

Both wait for Him. Lonely, slumped downward,
Trying to be tall, though every loss, every fall,
every hurt, just weakens the key.

Snapped, Cracked, Bruised
the broken heart
without the key you cannot proceed.
Where is the key?

You must discover yourself, but a tip I give,
It's not another woman's son, or another sister's brother.

Unfaithfully Yours

Too long married
To one who tarried
between righteousness and sin.
Man, ever failing to stand
Contend with temptation and sin.

Too long trying, too long crying,
because the church says pray, procreate and stay.
He'll change, God can. Wait!
Do not deviate from the vows you've made.
However, much the pain and the strain.

Trapped. Too long dependent on the little finances given,
the lies, always trying, ever-dying.
till your self-esteem is a long-lost dream.
As he plunges again head-first into the next episode of sin.

You can begin anew, and if need be alone
without the one who has hurt you so.
Just take one step and He will, take two.

Crossroads: My Forbidden Fruit

"Consumed," he said. "Not I," I replied.
I then thought, obsessed at best, lust if you must,
But then,
We touched!

I lied, to deny the acute attraction buried inside.

For I know him in the dark of my heart.
I see him in the deep of my sleep.
I smell him day and night.
That clean, fresh scent of masculinity that I want,
I see. I need.

Dare I defy the known truth that hovers in the
recesses of my mind? Is it greed?
Should I proceed, for I've sinned in my heart, and
grieved that which readily defines me?
At best, this is a test!

Do I forfeit the peace within?

Sin? At what cost?

So much to gain.

Too much already lost.

Is the answer simply bittersweet retreat AKA defeat?

I question thee, now my true and dearest friend.

How do we proceed?

Steadfast One, you fill a void, you meet a need in me.

Again, I ask, what do we do? How do we proceed?

Frustration mounts and now, I find myself

in a place I thought I'd never be

And I see myself with eyes cast low without an element of peace.

Is it guilt or grief?

Can I separate one from the other?

It matters not for One did come to rightly

fill all voids and meet all needs.

Ashantee´ Me

Call Them, Tell Them, Show Them
Dispel the myths.
Dismiss the lies.
Why? Because they need to know.
Who else will show them?
Don't be repelled.
I know they rebelled.
Don't be enraged.
I know they've engaged in much sin, from without and within.

Why sacrifice? Why give?
It is His way, not mine.
Don't harbor the pain, the shame of rejection.
With the Son comes a new day, a new way.

The door is open. The steps are not steep, not far.
Walk to them, through them.

The warrior within is called to act, and act now.

The Gift

Who can deny the power inside, the love that
denied long life, self-pride, personal wealth
in an attempt to provide destructive man with
an invitation towards salvation?
Who can ignore the passion, the pro-action, the
focus to ride the mare of death yet untried.
None but the Lamb of God could defy at once
and deny Death's Power, and Hell's Grip.

One Man, One Death, One Gift.

Why Sing?

I too, know why the captured bird sings.
He alone hears the pitch of the death knell
and the freedom bell ringing.

He alone has discovered the key, as long as he sings he lives, he
breathes, and there is an opportunity to be delivered and set free.

Exhume the Living before Dying the captured bird sings.
Free me! I want a chance to live, to fly away, to praise my King.

The Creator meant for all to be free, but the
choices we make dictate the life we lead.
Captive/Impoverished, So Many.
Does the captured one who hasn't the freedom to
go, continue to sing, to know his spirit and his soul
cannot be confined or controlled? He is free!

He, too, must discover as the captured bird did New Life,
Freedom in the Spirit, and the Joy that only His love can bring.

Opened Eyes Tell No Lies

You'll befriend me.

You'll sleep with me.

But

You will not support me, or acknowledge the truth.

You will not change your path.

Respect took a hit on that Friday nigh;

Yet I love you still, but Great Strength, no Depth

Little Faith, Heavy Laden has lain to wake another mistake.

Man, you are who you shall be, and though I
understand, commitment is part of me.

Pulling teeth to speak is no way to greet, fundamental obvious truth.

I'll leave soon.
You will stay.
Perhaps that's how it will end.

You care not enough to admit the truth. I care not enough to bend.

Old Fears/ Black Tears

Are her tears but salt for her wounds or cleansing for her call?
I believe that this challenge will not serve to break her, rather it will
help shape her, make and direct her through her grief to His Peace.
Where there is Relief.
I have often found that the measure of a man or
woman is not in what they say they'll do, but in that
which they do through the fears and the tears.

Two Left Feet

My two left feet and me can't move forward or retreat.
They're stuck in a place I'd rather not be.

Too tired to press, when they do move,
It's toward defeat, the wrong way.
They have a mind of their own, but they do not
think; they want, demand, and desire.
They're driven, limping, only getting by.

Perhaps, the bunions, flat-feet, and corns
represent more than just bad feet.
Is it manifested sin from within? Or tarrying at the sign
marked "DO NOT ENTER IN!" RETREAT.

Grief-stricken, I look for relief from the
wayward path of my two left feet.

Time to change, to re-arrange my priorities, my
mind, to govern the steps of my feet and me.

They must walk correctly, one left and one right.
Proceeding by Faith not Sight, not prompted by
emotions or selfish thoughts that slither up my spine
and remain trapped in my mind where
I see anger, jealousy, and deceit.

I speak freely now of my two left feet.
Now one left, and one right walking as they should be.

The Learned Way

When I was a thief

Then I was a liar

Impaled on a stake of fate and desire.

My wants and needs ruled my thoughts and deeds.

I did what I saw from when I did crawl.

I was not tamed or taught, I did not mature.

I just grew scarred and hard on the merry-go-round of getting

over and getting by frequently, hurting whoever got in the way.

I am me, but am I you too?

What am I now to do?

Continue to embrace the killing stake, or choose the path to freedom

and healing where I am no longer a now thief or a then liar?

Midnight

Ousted, but not alone, I moan.

The tragedies of my life, dark-hombre, take flight.

I have not lost my ethnicity, my roots, my right to be,

But the years have taken a toll.

I've not have one to have, to hold.

Nighttime seems yet to unfold in a rhythmic cycle, so dark, dank,

and cold.

Choices I've made, plans gone astray, and

emptiness so deep, I can no longer mask,

So I eat and sleep to control the rage that seeps

through the cracks in my soul.

Trapped am I day and night, try as I might, I cannot escape

the mistakes that linger in my head and my heart.

I am pigeon-holed in a life without a covering

at the gate of midlife,

Waiting and wanting,

Dying slowly inside in the midnight of my life.

Bordello

Who sold you?
What hurt you?
Who betrayed you?
Who suffered you
to ransom yourself for cost and lost?

Who stole your heart?
Humans trafficking, it seems, is still a means
to the Daddy, your pimp of despair.

Do you dare leave?
Do you care enough to discover or retrieve your
voice, your freedom, stand against captivity?

Do you know of the well?
Fresh Water dwells there to cleanse and dispel
All that clings and rings
Of your shame and pain.

Open your heart, your eyes to the truth not more deceitful lies.

You matter and captive birds can fly!

Addicted

I do not have a physical dependency,
on alcohol or drugs but
I too am addicted.

I did not choose the ways of this world
(for I was kept by a power higher than myself) but
I too am addicted.

I did not become a statistic, of the 70's or 80's but
I too am addicted.

Addicted to happier yesterdays,

And memories of good times long gone.

Addicted to continual pain, disappointment and trauma.

Addicted to a mindset that heretofore, worked in my life.

Addicted to silent frustration.

Addicted to expected betrayal rather than

eventual success and deliverance.

How do I shake this habit?

AA won't do.

NA can't help.

Encouraging Words supply but temporarily relief.

Who can help me?

Or must I remain addicted.

A Voice Silenced

The death of a voice.

The burial of a choice.

A mind apprehended

by confusion.

But

A gift still in tack.

Remembered not dismembered by time.

Still defined by holiness, truthfulness and

righteousness, Peace is sublime.

Happy

Happy to be me,
Happier yet to be free,
Happy to finally, see what I can do, what I can be.

Happy to know that I have grown to overcome great adversity.
Happy to learn the truth, see the proof, the Word can bring.
Happy to see the sun, lose the fear, no longer forced to run.

Happy to see my sisters experience the transformation,
the open-ended conversations.
New Birth, their value and worth.
Happy, Happy at last on seeing the opportunities.

www.ingramcontent.com/pod-product-compliance
Lightning Source LLC
Chambersburg PA
CBHW050342290526
45785CB00006B/2606